A Critical Historical Analyses of the International Political Economy

Mendel Tristan Pearl M.A.

ISBN: 197433953X
ISBN-13: 978-1974339532

DEDICATION

I would like to dedicate this book to my mom, grandmother
and stepdad
Who helped me along the way. I would like to thank them for
giving me the guidance and assist in this process.

CONTENTS

ACKNOWLEDGMENTS

I would like to acknowledge my mom, grandmother and step-dad for helping and encouraging me with this project. Especially my mom who was there to give much-needed support.

Abbreviations

APSR	American Political Science Review
GPE	Global Political Economy
IMF	International Monetary Fund
IO	International Organisations
IPE	International Political Economy
ipe	international political economy
IR	International Relations
LSE	London School of Economics
MC	Multinational Companies
MO	Multinational Organisations
NATO	North Atlantic Treaty Organisation
NIPE	New International Political Economy
NGO's	Non-Governmental Organisations
OEP	Open Economic Politics
OIPE	Old International Political Economy
PE	Political Economy

RBQ	Really Big Question
RIPE	Review of International Political Economy
UCLA	University of California, Los Angeles
UCSD	University of California, San Diego
UN	United Nations
US	United States
USA	United States of America
USSR	Union of Soviet Socalist Republics
UK	United Kingdom
WB	World Bank
WP	World Politics
WPE	World Political Economy
WWI	World War I (1914-1918)
WWII	World War II (1939-1945)

"IPE can be best defined as a set of interrelated problems. The IPE problematique contains a set of international and global challenges that cannot be merely perceived or analysed as just International politics or just International Economics. These problems fall substantially in the ever expanding field of the International Political Economy.

-What is the International Political Economy? An   excerpt from an article by Michael Veseth

Introduction: International Political Economy (IPE) A Historical Context

This corpus will explore the many aspects concerning the historical background of IPE, beginning with the debate between the International Political Economy (IPE) vs. International Relations (IR) from 1971-1990. Notable debates will include discourses around the New International Political Economy (New IPE) or NIPE and the Old International Political Economy (Old IPE) or OIPE from 1990-present and also explore questions about the landscape of IPE as a subfield. It is essential to come up with a comprehensive analysis to understand how IPE has evolved from a precisely nuanced and historical point of view. Also, the discourse on the British and American patterns of reasoning confirms the complexity of issues of IPE from 2007. The debates between the two modes of thought still endure today.

International Political Economy emerged from the doctrine of International Relations in 1971. International Relations is mainly known for its disciplinary struggles and "Great Debates" that identified four particular theories/inquiries that were set towards the end of World War I in 1918 culminating in the 1940's at the peak of World War II (WWII). The initial debate was held on the eve of war in 1939 (WWII) entitled Realism vs. Idealism. In this discussion, realism was a reaction against the utopian fantasy of idealism. President Woodrow Wilson, an idealist, wanted to disarm all nations after the great war of 1918. Realists saw the state of nature as being chaotic and recognised the importance of security in International Relations. The second debate arose in the 1960's between traditionalism and behaviouralism. Behaviouralist promoted the more rigorous scientific approach based on facts. The traditionalist defended the more interpretive historical approach through chronological and historical interpretation. The third debate within IR comprises the "Inter-Paradigm Debate", which took place in the 1970's between the Neo-realist and Neo-liberalist. Neo-liberalist believed in the international cooperation of nation states. Neo-realism views power as more important than cooperation. The fourth argument is the rationalist and reflectivist school of thought which arose during the 1980's and 1990's. Rationalist believes in the importance that multinational organisations play in the world order. Rationalist point to the importance of the United Nations. Reflectivist looks at assumptions, biases and commitments. This debate proceeds on with the epistemology of the field of study of International Relations. All the debates have an extraordinary significance on how IR expanded throughout the twentieth century and how it would represent a crucial role in the establishment and evolution of what would become known as the IPE.

The IPE is a new subfield within social sciences and was originated with Susan Strange, a renowned British scholar. During the 70s, Strange wrote an article on *International Politics and Economics* where she raised concerns about the varying rates of change within the international political structure, the impacts of these different rates of change in the world, and inter-country relationships (Strange, 1970). The decade of the 1970's witnessed significant political, economic and strategic evolutions that would have long-lasting ramifications. Susan Strange expressed grave concerns about the crisis of the Cold War along with her colleagues. The Cold War was between the US and its Western Partners NATO (North Atlantic Treaty Organisation) and the USSR (The Union of Soviet Socialist Republics) and its Eastern Allies the Warsaw Pact. The IPE evolved from IR during the peak of the Cold War. At the time some changes were apparent to researchers like Susan Strange who believed that a new discipline of study was imminent to deal with these constantly evolving changes. These transformations included multinational firms that began operations in several countries globally. Other alterations included the significant roles that some particular international agencies like the UN and NATO began to achieve. The period of the Cold War proved to be a crucial one that impacted the field of the IPE to what it is currently. The Cold War was an important case study into the ever-increasing interconnectedness of the international political economy.

Beginning in the 1970's, the economic system known as Bretton Woods was coming to an end. This was an agreement established by the United States and its allies in 1944, concerning an international monetary and financial order created after the defeat of Nazi Germany. In 1945 the United States emerged as the only capitalist nation with both the economic and military might to help rebuild Europe and Asia following World War II. In 1971 President Richard Nixon decided to exclude the US from the Bretton Woods treaty. Strange heavily criticised that judgement voicing concern, that the withdrawal would affect the prevailing world order. Strange feared this new world of global finances, independent of states and industrial productions that had begun to emerge. In 1977, one of the most influential interpretations of IPE was characterised by Joan Spero (1977) who argued that the study of IPE had been ignored in the 20th century. Joan Spero (1977) claimed that politics and economics had been separated from each other and that the IPE had been broken down into international politics and international economics (1977, pp.1-2). It was this understanding of a divided and secluded hypothesis that some suggest catapulted IPE into a field of study.

During the early years of the International Political Economy, several key researchers besides Susan Strange stood out as notable. Among them were: Cooper (1968); Baldwin (1971); Keohane (1972); Kindleberger (1972); and Spero (1977). These academics comprise the foundation of the International Political Economy. This may be the first occasion when IPE was authored or genuinely referenced. IPE intellectuals, like Susan Strange, maintained that previous studies of IR had solely emphasised diplomacy, politics and law. On the same note, neoclassical economics was blamed for being abstract and ahistorical. Basing its argument mainly on historical sociology and economic history, IPE scholars suggested an integration of economics with political analysis. This disturbed both the Marxist and liberal IPE intellectuals who disputed the dependence of Western social science on the regional state as a basis of analysis and fought for the reinstatement of the international system.

After analysing the future of IPE, Robert Cox concluded that:

The social impetus is not to be perceived of as existing entirely within states. Certain social forces may supersede state boundaries and global structures which can be understood as the alignment of state power. The globe can be perceived as an evolution of interacting social factors within certain nations. This may be referred to as a political, economic view of the world: power can be conceptualised as evolving from social forces and not regarding accumulated material goods (Cox, 1996. p.4).

The author's above definition would shift IPE from perceiving States as major actors in the global economy to those different powers that tend to ignore states.

A concern for the discipline of IPE according to Pepsinky (2013) is the focusing solely on individuals. However, the fact of the matter is that personal-level information can only be used as a complement, and never a replacement, of the aggregate-level research on the world's political economy. The big challenge is how to apply findings from research studies into the current theoretical discourse and what to do when outcomes do not complement each other (Pepsinky, 2013. p. 438). The IPE comprises the interrelationships of daily changes that exist amongst certain groups, for instance, governments, businesses, and other forces across the global arena. IPE takes into account various elements of the world economy such as taxes, trades, tariffs and plays an essential role in the international political economy; Global Political Economy (GPE); the Political Economy (PE); and the World Political Economy (WPE). The main reason why the field of IPE appears to be confusing is as a result of abbreviations such as IPE, GPE, PE, WPE, which are usually used interchangeably.

The IPE considers the overall political economy, and analyses not only states but other important actors. These players include individuals, businesses, (both public and private companies) think tank and political parties. This is what separates the field of the International Political Economy from its sister's areas within the Social Science discipline like International Relations. IPE is uniquely suited to study these complex individual actors.

The areas of focus for International Political Economy scholars are extensive and varied. While states are still an area of research, they are not the primary focus. Instead, researchers within the field look at local entities like cities and counties which include interest groups and lobbyist. Companies both public and private are also analysed and studied by scholars of IPE.

Two distinctions need to be made about the International Political Economy. First, there is the difference between International Political Economy (IPE) and international political economy (ipe). The international political economy in lowercase format deals with the real world economy. The International Political Economy in upper case format deals strictly with the academic community. Second, it is sometimes referred to as the Global Political Economy (GPE). This gets confusing when some authors interchange the

International Political Economy (Academic) with the Global Political Economy (Academic).

The need to put the International Political Economy into a series of debates has been lacking in IPE literature. Other Social Sciences like International Relations are known for its debates. This thesis puts the International Political Economy into three distinct debates that began in the 1970's. These debates are an important part of the evolution of the field of IPE. Since its early days, the International Political Economy has grown into its distinct field with its journals and academic discipline. Within that short time, the International Political Economy has distinguished itself as a recognised discipline with its areas of investigations within the global political economy.

Chapter I: Debate I: Is IPE a subfield of IR?

Is IPE, in fact, a sub-discipline of IR or an independent field? IPE developed "as an interdisciplinary study in the early 70s and was born out of disillusionment with existing research in the fields of IR and IE. Serious work on IR research focused on the causes and impacts of war between states, marginalising issues of economic importance and their effect on international political relations (Baker, 2005 p. 4).

According to Strange (1994), the field of IPE was not an exclusive self-governing area of study, but dependent upon IR. In her article on *State's and Markets* the same wanted to find out the reason nation-states perpetuated war whereas it was apparent that the economic benefits of war would never outstrip the economic costs of continuing the war (Strange, 1994). That is the essence of IR, nations and why they prefer to wage war. IPE, answers the question raised by Stange (1994) on the reason various states cannot regulate and stabilise a global financial system which is, in fact, imperative to the real economy. IPE, therefore, is a discipline that delves to investigate political and economic matters in the global arena more than does IR. While this might be the case, Strange furthermore looked at the relationship with IR as having been manipulated by the American intellectuals and has been permeated by covert value judgements and theories based on American experience perspective (Strange, 1994).

When trying to understand IPE, one can discern certain limitations within the discipline. Susan Strange expressed her views on these constraints. She articulates three such restrictions:

Primarily, the limitations are as a result of the history of three basic social sciences: Economics, political science, and international relations. Both of the first two were developed early in the twentieth century that state frontiers split different political and financial systems so they could be studied and analysed for all practical purposes in separation from each other, or else relatively as if they were separate species of animals. The third, IR, was so centred on challenges, of war and peace that it had problems answering any other questions other than that of the new world order (Strange, 1994).

Strange sees the limitations of Politics, Economics, and IR as justifications as to why the IPE is its own field.

Per Barry Gills, views two aspects of IPE as a distinct and unique discipline:

First of all, IPE commences its enquiry by opposing the divorcing of 'politics' from 'economics' and the false notion that these are distinct fields of behaviour each with separate rules and attributes, to be perceived through different concepts and principles. Secondly, IPE discards the 'regional' and the 'international', or between the 'inside' and the 'outside' of international borders. Rather, the author seeks to establish a structure of analysis that allows individuals to scrutinise the co-determination and co-constituency of the regional and the international. The regional and the international are thus as 'intimate' as the political and the economic as elements of social power. (Gill, 2001 p.234).

These two points are crucial in comprehending the differences which are evident between IPE and IR. Politics and economics are intertwined and highly rely on one another. The fact that IPE centres on politics and economics are an essential element of the field.

A recurring theme in the IPE is Globalisation. Globalisation is a critical aspect of IPE as it delves into how people, institutions and other legal entities function on a global scale. With the ever-growing interconnectedness of business and international trade, this becomes an important factor. Especially during the 1970's and 1980's, other non-state actors, appeared and assumed vital roles which IR overlooked. The parts of International Organizations (IO), Multinational Organisations (MO), Non-Governmental Organisations (NGO's) are high performing actors that are exclusive to the international political economy. The idea that IR is not suited or is criticised as inept to handle non-state actors has been argued "as hardly astounding given that the academics came from the field of IR. Their disciplinary foundation naturally led to an emphasis on big questions about the shape and dynamics of the international system (Walter, 2009). The Global Political Economy as a field looks at many aspects of the world economy.

The International Political Economy looks and:

Starts from an awareness of the centrality of perspective in setting the problematic which is often more important than the answers. Because what is asked and answered nearly always determines the answers. An IPE problematic also asks the questions about the relationship that exists between politics and economics at the global level and the nexus between the regional policies and processes *(Tooze, 1984)*.

IPE, begins with the simple question by asking what is the global political economy?   While the answers are relevant, the issue is vital. IPE explores matters of states, be it Unitary (The United Kingdom, Israel) or Federal, (The United States, Germany, Switzerland, Austria). Humanitarian Organisations such as the United Nations, International Monetary Fund, World Bank and many other international organisations (Walmart, Boeing), are major players in the political economy. These shifts the economics from state players to the corporate agencies within those states. Researchers and academics seek to address   problems   by   considering   four   classes   of explanatory factors:

To begin with, the distribution of international power, particularly the role of a hegemonic nation. Secondly, the framework, function, and impact of multinational institutions. Thirdly, the effect of nonmaterialist ideologies and beliefs. Fourthly, is the impact of regional policies (Milner, 1998).

IPE can, therefore, be perceived as a field that acknowledges all work for which international economic elements are a primary cause or effect (Frieden & Martin,

2003). Lastly, the discipline of the International Political Economy is a multidisciplinary social science field that interrogates, analyses, and suggest amendments in the process of financial flows and political leadership that crosses over and goes beyond national boundaries'' (Milner, 2008).

One of the popular reading material that began showing up in the 80's in the US was *The Political Economy of International Relations* book by Robert Gilpin. Whereas it is known as IR in the States, the author mentions IPE and labels it as "a series of inquiries to be looked into by utilising different strategies and theoretical perspectives". In 2000, a different IPE textbook titled *the International Political Economy: Perspectives on Global Power and Wealth*, written by Jeffrey Frieden and David Lake portrayed IPE as "the transaction of monetary elements and legislative matters on the planet ". This quote seems to take after that of Strange.

The IPE appears to deal with matters that international relations cannot. According to Amy Verdun (2003), IPE was an extended version of IR. The field would look at not only the communications between state actors but other notable actors, especially, the transnational and local players, for example, the national and non-state players (Verdun, 2003). The only issue with IR is that it is overly restricted in what it can handle, about what happens with various actors, other than countries on the global arena. IPE, whereas it might seem to be expansive, it has looked into these different players and has evaluated their significance.

The distinctions of IPE to IR is that IPE concentrates more on globalisation. Another important angle that isolates the two fields:

"In a nutshell, then, our objective is to reconsider the elements of the political parameters within the IPE as a contribution to the expansion of a genuinely multidisciplinary field of study— one that rejects the idea of privileging the political, the economic and in fact the international. Our claim as editors, even though not essentially shared by all the immediate contributors, is that just as all elements of the IPE might be understood as having international and economic implication on existence. That all elements of the IPE can be perceived as political, nevertheless, is not to argues that their specificity is exhausted by such an explanation, nor that it is always imperative to account for them in such terms. (Hay, 2007, p.10).

IPE is, therefore, more capable of breaking down the global economy since it checks the social perspectives of the political and financial parts of the worldwide political economy.

Geoffrey Underhill describes the International Political Economy as a field that is currently in

"A revival and realigning of the study of 'matters International' with the large convention of social science scholarship from the French Physiocrats going forward, such as Smith, Marx, Keynes, Polanyi, and the forerunners of the contemporary period. IPE found its space by investigating its roots and in building bridges with other social science fields. Besides, the process of developing the field was a shared venture. The growth of this area shows that it is deeply rooted in the intellectual movements which brought about the classical political economy and a range of modern social sciences and sub-disciplines (Underhill, 2000 p.7).

In the present-day period, it appears that numerous researchers concur that the area concentrates on a few investigations that are vital when contemplating the International Political Economy.   Per Balaam and Dillman (2014), there are four levels of study that make up the field, and it appears that most researchers concur:

"Global Level, which is the broadest and greatest level of investigation. The Interstate Level, which is how the relative parity of political, military, and monetary force between states influences the likelihood of war and participation. The State/Societal Level, because the focus narrows to performers inside states; Finally, The Individual Level, because capable individuals are essential also" (Balaam & Dillman, 2014).

These levels are pivotal in understanding IPE in the current connection of the late twentieth and twenty-first centuries.

While Denemark and O'Brien sorted out IPE as two fields as per Mario Telo a political scientist from Italy, the International Political Economy is not an independent field of study, as Telo portrays IPE as being perceived as a sub-field of International Relations. Telo notices that the International Political Economy is an interdisciplinary way to deal with universal life that supports the investigation of both financial and political connections on a worldwide scale (Telo, 2009). Robert Cox also stated that the International Political Economy is not its field. IPE rather is a standing framework that reacts to the interruption of another social gathering by including another rank, so the global political economy is by all accounts discovering its put in a regular scholastic request as another sub-field of a sub-field—IPE joins International Organization (IO) journal along the hall of IPE" (Cox, 1981). Cox while recognising that IPE is picking up significance, really goes above and beyond Denemark and O'Brien and proclaims a twofold sub-field along IR. This thought of IPE as being bound by international relations does not show up outside the United States.

Robert Tooze in analysing Susan Strange work noted that three properties make IPE independent from IR. These three attributes are:

"First of all, power in society is the essence of the political economy. Political power can be exercised in various ways, especially in structures as opposed to indirect relations with entities. Secondly, the distinction between 'politics' from 'economics', with their disciplinary superstructures developed upon this separation, makes a convincing analysis of political economy almost infeasible, and when applied produces inappropriate analysis as the basis for inept policy. Thirdly, a sole focus on the state can negative consequences and can also give a flawed perception of politics that is not adequate to offer an understanding of the human condition. The most significant body not acknowledged by state-centric IR is the corporation, and the fundamental elements of nance/credit

and technology are unrecognised by traditional 'politics'"
(Tooze, 2000 p. 3).

These three findings that Tooze discovered considering Susan Strange work as critical in stating fundamentally that these two fields are different. Tooze alongside Strange unequivocally advocates that IPE, not a sub-field but rather a free, independent field outside of IR.

This debate is between IPE literature that is intimately connected with the field of International Relations (IR/IPE), versus IPE scholarship that draws more of the classic traditions of political economy (PE) (Broome, 2014). The above idea is yet another side that the field of the International Political Economy is an area which remains controversial. The globalisation problématique is quite different from the traditional state-centered concerns of IR, which is why some scholars consider IPE a distinct academic discipline, not just a sub-field of International Relations. As a process driven by the global expansion of production and finance, globalisation forces us to look at the interrelationships between politics, business, culture, technology, the environment, and migration.

The growing prominence of IPE is one result of the continuing breakdown of boundaries between economics, politics, and other social science disciplines. Increasingly, the most pressing problems that scholars and policy-makers confront are those that can best be understood from a multidisciplinary, interdisciplinary, or transdisciplinary point of view. The International Political Economy is an area of investigation, a particular range of questions, and a series of assumptions about the nature of the international system and how it should be understood" (Tooze, 1984). Hence "the focus of study becomes the causes and effects of the world market economy …the significance of the global economy for domestic economies" (Gilpin, 1987). The content of the International Political Economy may have been the most significant in the last three decades for the development of certain concepts and approaches (Ravenhill, 2009).

Chapter II: Debate II: Old IPE vs. New IPE

This section will examine the debate between the old school of the International Political Economy (Old IPE) and the new school known as Open Economic Politics (OEP) or New International Political Economy (NIPE). Old International Political Economy of the 1960's and 1970's delved into the political consequences of financial interdependence in a critically loose but a creative way (Keohane, 2009 p. 34). A different school of thought within IPE referred to as the Open Economic Politics sprung up during the 1980's (Lake, 2009). The New International Political Economy or Open Economic Politics as conceptualised in the open economy politics approach (OEPA), is more stringent and has the virtue of assimilating both the comparative and international political economy into a standard structure (Keohane, 2009 p. 37). This research field has significantly evolved over the past two decades as the dominant paradigm in the field (Rho, 2016) of the International Political Economy. Open Economic Politics is fully recognised within the U.S. and throughout the world (Rho, 2016). This "research field looks into the source of societal inclinations over tariffs, economic and exchange rate laws, and the flow of investments. It evaluates how the structure of regional political institutions, for instance, type of regime, electoral and party structures, veto players, and central bank autonomy, aggregate and make over preferences into policy results (Oatley, 2011 p. 1).

Old IPE witnessed the profound transformation in the international political economy during the twentieth century. During the decades of the 1970's and 1980's scholars of the old IPE witnessed the end of Bretton Woods in 1971 when President Nixon pulled the United States out of the Gold Standard; a year later in 1972, Nixon made his famous trip to Red China. 1973 witnessed the Arab-Israel War followed by the Arab oil embargo which in turn caused economic stagflation, especially in the United States. The 1970's also witnessed the beginning of the end of the Vietnam War, with the Paris Peace Treaty in 1973 with the political ramification of America's military withdrawal that same year. 1973 also saw the United Kingdom join the European Economic Zone. Two years later in 1975, South Vietnam fell. Towards the end of the 1970's IPE scholars experienced further economic chaos with the 1978-1979 Iranian Revolution, the invasion of

Afghanistan by the U.S.S.R. in 1979 and the Iran-Iraq war.

The 1970's also experienced the emergence of Multinational Companies (MC) and Globalisation. These were companies that would have headquarters in one country but operations in multiple countries throughout the globe. Such companies included Wal-Mart, Boeing, IBM, Dell, Ford, SAMSUNG to name a few. Moreover, would play important roles in shaping the global political economy.

The 1980's saw further political and economic crisis. The Iran-Iraq War and the invasion of Afghanistan by the U.S.S.R were still ongoing causing an economic crisis. Latin American countries beginning in 1982 with Mexico, the countries of Central America and South America experienced their financial crisis. The crisis finally eased in the 1988-1989 when the International Monetary Fund (IMF) began preparing bailouts. 1988-1989 saw the beginning of the end of the Cold War with the U.S.S.R pulling out of Afghanistan and the end of the Iran-Iraq War. The fall of the Berlin Wall in 1989 was a surprise to many scholars. Suffice to say no one predicted that the Soviet Union would fall towards the end of the 1980's and early 1990's. The decade of the 1980's ended with Revolutions sweeping throughout Europe and the world, that would be known as the "Revolutions of 1989".

The Open Economic Politics approach "reminds scholars that even international institutions are but one part of a broader political process and that their role and effects can be fully understood in that context" (Lake, 2009). To focus than on just the key actors in the international political arena is an error on mainstream IPE. Open Economic Politics suggests Rho (2016) also looks at individuals such as ordinary citizens. Deducing this theory per OEP suggests that it:

"Rests on the assumption that the policy preferences of individuals and groups reflect economic self-interest. Each individual or group presumably wants the system that would maximise their real income. To determine which policy would serve this goal, analysts consult economic theory; they use economic models to infer how policies would affect an actor's income, given the player's endowments and role in the global economy (Rho, 2016 p. 86).

One must realise that individual citizens are just as important to the international political economy.

Since Open Economic Politics has only emerged since the 1990's, most of the research has focused on a limited source of articles. While the literature has expanded, one can see the limits that are placed on Open Economic Politics research. At the beginning, Open Economic Politics studied the effects of trade and finance on the global political system. (Morrison, 2011).

When the New International Political Economy (NIPE) emerged in the 1990's, NIPE scholars witnessed what some would call "*The End of History*". The 1990's were a time of political turmoil throughout the world with the collapse of the U.S.S.R and its communist satellite countries in Eastern Europe beginning in 1990. Political turmoil began with the swift pullout of Soviet troops from Eastern Europe and the German unification of West Germany and the East Germany. Two years later in 1993, the former Czechoslovakia would split in two creating the new countries of the Czech Republic and the Slovak Republic. Towards the end of the 1990's NIPE scholars witnessed and analysed the Asian economic crisis and the impeachment trials happening in the United States. The Asian economic sent ripples throughout the Asian economies that were similar to those of the Latin American Crisis the previous decade.

Open Economic Politics is mainly found within the American version of IPE. The IPE has now moved to younger generational scholars within OEP of the American School (Hobson, 2011). As Hobson (2011) suggests, OEP is very American and Eurocentric. Open Economic Politics starts by analysing the different actors within a certain society within the international political economy (Lake, 2008). OEP like IPE looks at other none-state actors: enterprises, industries or factors of production that might be expected to share similar interests.

The Old IPE in contrasts to the New Open Economic Politics per Lake focuses on two distinct questions. These issues are First when, why and how do countries choose to accept transborder movement of goods and services, capital, and people?. Secondly, how does integration (or lack of it) into the international economy impact the interests of individuals, industries, factors of production, or nations and, in turn, domestic policies? (Lake, 2009b). These are the questions that per Lake separates IPE from OEP.   While OEP focuses on national actors, three further criteria must be tackled:

"First, they examine how local institutions affect the ability of political actors to construct the rules and norms governing

interdependent relations and thus offer a source of asymmetric power. Second, they explore how interdependence alters domestic political institutions through processes of diffusion, trans-governmental coordination and extraterritorial application and in turn change the national institutions mediating internal debates on globalisation. Third, they study the shifting boundaries of political contestation through which sub-state actors affect decision-making in foreign jurisdictions. Hence, they challenge prevailing notions that interdependence, domestic institutions, or interest group distributions are static or exogenous (Farrell, 2014 p. 2-3).

This is the foci that Open Economic Politics researches and investigates. While IPE does not ignore these actors, these actors are an important area of research for scholars of OEP. Lake (2009b) goes on to report that the major divide within this school of thought is between the Ricardo-Viner or particular factors theory of international trade, which hypothesises that, usually, capital and labour are constant, in specific occupations and, hence, will tend to have like interests over fiscal policy. The Heckscher-Ohlin-Samuelson (HOS) model of international trade, which hypothesises that all factors are variables across occupations within countries and, thus, capital and labour will have conflicting interests. Further Open Economic Politics supports an overly frugal and positivist/quantitative methodology that aims to develop 'scientifically rigorous' research, preferably through econometric analysis. Indeed, this econometric tendency of American IPE has escalated in geometric fashion in the last two decades" (Hobson, 2011).

Open Economic Politics, unlike the International Political Economy, is based on what Lake (2009b) refers to as methodological reductionism. OPE's methodological reductionist approach,

"Makes it suitable for the provision of comparatively precise understanding. To begin with, the mid-range concepts that it develops helps scholars to develop a well specified causal relationship about regional politics this enables researchers to change the basis of their empirical analysis from a single qualitative case study to quantitative studies where a meaningful number of observations allows for the utilisation of statistical tests (Oatly, 2011 p. 8-9).

Both Open Economic Politics and the International Political Economy looks at domestic actors. However, unlike IPE, OPE delves further into local players. The Open Economic Politics system investigates domestic actors that are separate from their global peers. Open Economic Politics is evident in this research analysis in two journals, *International Organization* (IO) and the

American Political Science Review (APSR) (Oatley, 2011).

In analysing the different stages of domestic institutions within Open Economic Politics research, three steps can be deferred.

"First, a relevant domestic feature is the relative strength of political intermediaries, that is interest groups and political parties.   Second, the national institutional architecture matters. Officials – both democratic and undemocratic – want to remain in office and thus aggregate competing interests in a manner meant to further this goal. In the third stage of OEP, countries negotiate with one another over the solution of international problems, the implementation policies, and the creation and functioning of international institutions (Owen, 2016 p.181).

This is what differentiates Open Economic Politics from the old International Political Economy.   There are several features that IPE neglects, 'intermediaries', 'interest groups' and 'political parties' as well as 'Officials' of countries.   Another feature is the commonality of the two when they analyse the international problems. OEP,

"Is triply reductionist in that: first, ontologically, it focuses on domestic economic interest groups as the core independent

variable. Second, these groups are defined exogenously according to purely economistic/rationalist criteria; and third, epistemologically, OEP rests on a highly reductionist and quantitative/positivist methodology (Hobson, 2011).

An important and interesting note is that IPE scholars especially NIPE scholars failed to predict the 2008 global financial crisis. The IPE in today's world, particularly after the 2007-2008 global recession has transformed even more than the states elements of the international political economy. According to Mosley and Singer (2010), three pressing topics of concern have been raised:

"The first one is the influencers of cross-national changes in financial regulation. The second ones are the patterns of collaboration and disunity within global regulatory agencies and the engagement of emerging-market nations in these bodies.The third is the relationship between individual firms-as-political-players and public policy regulations. (Mosley & Singer, 2010).

The global financial crisis was not only a pivotal moment for the global political economy but the field of IPE. IPE scholars were criticised as not being able to foresee the outcome that proved to be the worst financial crisis since the Great Depression of the 1930's.   As Mosley &

Singer (2009) stated scholars of IPE "are generally not in the business of predicting financial crises or recessions".

How this relates to IPE scholarship is that no word was mentioned about the crisis in IPE journals. No one predicted the financial crisis beforehand or expected the financial crisis of 2007-2009 to be as severe as it was. Neither OIPE nor NIPE predicted this crisis and both were at fault for failing to take this crisis seriously. However, what is interesting is that at this moment in time a debate was brewing in IPE that would cause considerable controversies.

Chapter III: Debate III: The Transatlantic Divide in IPE

The hullabaloo surrounding the field of IPE developed into a heated discourse in 2007. It has been thought that neither of the scholars from either side of the Atlantic held talks with one another, and for the most part, the intellectuals who subscribed to the British School of thought perceived the American School of thought as snobbish. For instance, Susan Strange gave her clear vision when she reported that the most important thing was come up with a standard method of evaluating the world economy that factors in students or reader choices and opens doors for more pragmatism. Secondly, Strange also suggested break down the walls dividing the uncompromising ideologies to encourage some communication and even constructive discourse between them (Strange, 1994). This analysis comprises what would end up becoming the divide or debate in the IPE.

Cohen (2007) reports that during the 1970's, numerous scholars met to form a new field of discipline in analysing the IPE and brainstorm on what theories and models fit. It seems that IPE was not unified with the split across the Atlantic from The US to the UK. According to   Cohen (2007), the contrast between American and British schools are so great the author justified both schools of thoughts from each other (Cohen, 2008. p. 198). The same author was surprised as to the reaction that followed his argument. A majority of the academics rubbished his work while a few supported him. It has been thought that it was through Cohen's work that the great debate began.

Cohen's explanation was not exactly as reported by two scholars who argued that argue that Cohen's claim in his RIPE essay was fundamentally flawed. The two authors argue that if he Cohen genuinely believed his explanation of the field based on his assertion, then his proposal for a reconciliation of the dissenting camps of American and British IPE on some possible neutral is a waste of time (Higgot & Watson. 2008).   This open discussion applies to the discipline of the global political economy that whereas moderately new, has grown to be important in conceptualising what IPE is. Higgott and Watson apparently both differ that there is any division between the two schools of thought,

The argument about the field of the IPE and its contribution to the Social Science is continuing. The American School of IPE has always been intergrated with the mainstream of IPE due to its popularity in the pages of the top rated International Relations Journals (IRJ). The predisposition of 'state of the discipline' studies to overly depend on interpretive or quantitative content analyses of high impact factor journals to have a deeper understanding of the field (Sharman & Weaver, 2013).

In assessing the American School, there are individuals such as Randall Germain, who do not agree with Cohen's ideologies about the American School. Germain severely disapproves of Cohens American School thesis, for instance,

"He rejects Cohen's depiction of the IPE from American school as fundamentally inaccurate and that Cohen's conceptualisation of the school sounds more like the Harvard School of thought. In German's opinion, IPE in America is a rich and a changing enterprise while Harvard school does not change. German further argues that IPE in America is extremely centralised and hierarchical, which gives the 'Harvard' school a larger latitude to influence the self-portrayal of the field and in some ways also its trajectory (German, 2009).

It appears then that Germain's point of contention with the American School is that it is only narrowed to one university. This notion that the American IPE is too parochial presents a problem in the US and North America that more universities need to have input on how IPE is studied and portrayed.

The argument that followed the rift between the American School and British School of IPE probably is questionable. Whereas it may seem apparent that there are two conflicting schools of thought, what defines them?

"A 'school' is characterised by high internal consistency and the marked difference with other 'schools'. After having reflected further, I concluded that the dichotomy is not very useful; in fact, I question whether the idea of constructing 'schools' in IPE is a good one. As a field IPE is variety, and it should continue to be. Pluralism is our comparative advantage, not a nuisance. Unlike neoclassical economics, it makes us able to view the real world as it is: varied, complex, dynamic and changing, producing disequilibria as much as equilibria. Moreover, if after all, we were to construct

'schools', doing it along geographical lines is a bad idea"
(Hveem, 2009).

It looks like that Hveem has an issue with the word "school" and that he does not think that it should be referred to when talking about the IPE. Besides, the field of IPE is extensive and dynamic to be merely limited to a particular school of thought. This open debate applies to the areas of the global political economy that even though it is relatively new, it has been found to be crucial in portraying what IPE is. Higgott and Watson apparently both disagree that there is any division between the schools because they recognise that it was imperative to raise the verbal exchange, that there is no partition.

Murphy and Nelson concur with Cohen and utilises his same words by saying that, "IPE partitioned between what we will reference an "English school". The other is the "American school" or the "International Organization (IO) school" of IPE, after the US journal that has been the essential site of its advancement. (Numerous British school researchers would likely incline toward the name "Basic IPE". An interesting perspective on the verbal confrontation between the transatlantic separation is figuring out whether Cohen is right.

The American School of IPE

The American School of the IPE came into being as a self-referential community of academics whose graduate research work was done at Harvard University in the 60's (Murphy et al., 2001). For a majority of the Political Scientist intellectuals in the U.S. the IPE is not perceived as a field, but rather a methodology of economics used in the analysis of political trends and institutions (Weingast, 2006).

According to a study conducted in 2006 of undergraduate IPE syllabi on Political Science at both public and private colleges in the entire US, it was found that almost two-thirds of the courses offered to reflect the various states and markets approach whereas only 10 percent adopted the globalisation approach (Paul, 2013). This particular study revealed how universities in the US focused on the power of States in the global arena. Also, noted, where IPE was initially limited to case studies or at best statistical outcomes based on small amounts of data, some of the best new research utilised a large number of samples and robust econometric applications (Lake, 2006).

Using the American School to define the IPE takes for granted the interrelationship in the global economy and that it can be evaluated in political terms, not simply as an economic concept (Cohen, 2007). Besides the IPE defined within the 'American' School is perceived as a continuation of IR. As per Gilpin (2001), "the interplay in the market and such influential players as states, international firms, and multinational organisations, as defined by the author take a state-centric approach to the matter.

The American school of thought and its ideology according to the *International Organization Journal* (IO) are assumed to be a rationalist one; that relationship between states are its typical "dietary staple"; members of this "species" are considered to have distinct formal tools and robust quantitative models (Dickens, 2006). It makes it possible for IO to disseminate information about the necessary aspects of the global political economy while at the same time digest it. Presently the American school model is becoming increasingly standardised. It appears to resemble nothing so much as the methodology used in neoclassical economics, characterised by the same predilection for positivist analysis, rigorous modelling, and where possible, organised collection and analysis of empirical data (Cohen, 2007). The *IO* is quite familiar with the American School particularly in IR which is the corner stone of American IPE.

For instance, according to Maliliniak and Tierney (2009), the literature on IPE focus comprise only of 13 percent of the total articles published since 1980. This is despite the fact that 30 percent of IR academics in the US reporting their primary field as IPE. Besides, during this time, the IPE's share of publications in the top 12 journals has been reported to vary from a high of 20 percent in 1984 and 1985 to a low of 5 percent in 1994. This shows that from the journals analysed; there is remarkable variation. Maliliniak and Tierney (2009) also argue that there is 37 percent of IPE publications since 1980 are available in the pages of IO, followed by International Studies Quarterly (ISQ) and World Politics containing 22 percent and 10 percent, respectively.

The American School in the US universities is famous for being particularly well considered in IPE. Some of these universities include Harvard, Berkeley, Princeton, U.C.S.D., and U.C.L.A. which usually mentions the American School at the Political Science Association Bar (Maliniak, 2009). As far as the school is concerned, ontology remains exclusively state-centric, placing the national governments above any other unit of interest (Cohen, 2007). In dealing with the British School, for example, Catherine Weaver depicts it, as left brained. In that, the British school's tendency to being more illuminating, observational and seemingly un-beholden to any particular arrangement of ontological assumptions or methodological limitations is more open to soliciting the primary concerns that empower its subscribers to anticipate dramatic transformation in the international economy (Weaver, 2009). The American school of thought as portrayed by Catherine Weaver is that being right brained. For instance, Weaver expresses that "the most important clarification for the present left-cerebrum identity of the American school of IPE stems from perceptions of the preparation and expert socialisation of graduate studies" (Weaver, 2009). Further, she goes on to say that the American School "appears as though they are coordinating graduates and preparing the US picked as an elective hemispherectomy – the persistent expulsion of the whole right mind. Keeping in mind the end goal to give vitality towards honing the specific elements of the left cerebrum (and maybe to keep the sort of individual cacophony that may incite epileptic scholarly conduct in their graduate understudies)" (Weaver, 2009). It is for sure an interesting relationship in that the American School, relates to the left cerebrum regarding breaking down the IPE.

At the point when managing the narrow-mindedness of the American School of IPE towards visible impact, Weaver says that the International Political Economy as an international field still displays the differing qualities of thought which Susan Strange prized. Inside the United States, this distinction is by all accounts vanishing. The homogenization of the International Political Economy of the development of a flexible chain of importance emphatically benefits one epistemology, one approach, and one worldview over others (Weaver, 2008). She further elucidates on the American framework that the rising American monoculture, as portrayed by numerous others on this particular issue, is merely the indication of Kuhnian advancement in sociology, wherein one methodology gets to be overwhelming a direct result of the apparent predominance of its outcomes. The monoculture today additionally is by all accounts the result of a focused scholarly environment in which we are constrained to live by the mantra of 'distribute or die" (Weaver, 2008).

When analysing at the American school of IPE, one can tell that it applies econometrics model, that there are some individuals already referred to as "economists" who can obviously do well with this field. However, if the American School IPE is playing politics using in the model, then there might be no value-added as Blyth (2009) claims. This is a fascinating point about the American school as it makes one wonder why the American School IPE seem to involve itself with what Blyth (2009) calls 'econometrics' while there is already a discipline devoted to economics. That is probably one of the controversial issues with the American School.

The British School of IPE

Susan Strange created the model as a substitute to the American School. Academics who are opposed to the American School of thought argues that the Critical theory methodology of the British School is more agreeable as it directs focus to the crunches and paradoxes that could be represented by changes in social, economic, and political systems (Cox, 2009). As a student at the London School of Economics (LSE), she concentrated on the subject area of IR. It has been said that Strange was an academic IR for years until one day she had a "divine manifestation" that something was revolutionising the current political system and the worldwide political economy. Strange believed that at this time her field of IR study was incompetent in investigating and evaluating these new transformations. She looked into new research that was not solely state-centric. The field of the International Political Economy soon emerged. However, it seems that while it was Strange's attempt to analyse the new changes that were occurring during the 1970's, the field of IPE was a byproduct of that endeavour.   Strange never actually intended to create an entirely new academic discipline.

By discerning the transformations in the IPE, the British School is distinctively qualified. From the various international agencies such as the International Monetary Fund (IMF), the World Bank (WB), the United Nations (UN), the European Union (EU), and NATO, one can better explain how these organisations function by using the British School. The numerous theories and files that culminate in the British School of IPE are understood to represent the high diversity that comprises the IPE.

The British School's leading journals are the *Review of International Political Economy (also known as* RIPE) and *New Political Economy* (also known as NPE) (begun in 1996). RIPE established in the early 1990's; was a conscious attempt to nullify all the schools of thought that stood up to the hegemony of hyper-liberalism according to Germann (2011). The British school perceives the state as simply one agent among several if states are to be considered they also evoke a deeper interest in normative concerns (Cohen, 2007). Also, the British school supports approaches that tend to be more historical and institutional and more interpretive in quality. Less traditional methodologies are preferred to take into account the school's wider range of analytical matters (Cohen, 2007).

Whereas the American School emphasises on State Hegemony, the British School tends to be more concerned with what Cohen refers the ' Big Question' (RBQ): for instance, where is the planet going and how can people impact its direction? About the ' Big Question' that was noted by Cohen, Mark Blythe (2009) goes even further. He reports that IPE is after all a complex open entropic adaptive structure with disequilibrium subtleties and nonlinear dynamics. Then and only then, might one as well be sometimes right about the RBQ rather than precisely right about the small details that may change with time. The objective of the British and those who subscribe to the British school might seem less practical than strategic. It is all about how a state can best manage trade policy or fiscal policy given the prevailing conditions (Cox, 2009). This School goes even further and utilises various analysis to investigate the International Political Economy. One may, in fact, ask whether IPE considers the stresses and contradicting issues within the whole myriad of societies and states that results in a transformation of existing structures in ways that might be either adversely divisive and conflictual or, more equitable and peaceful (Cox, 2009). This kind of IPE thought directly contravenes the doctrine of the American School.

In the British School, academics in the British style help to make up for such flaws with their intellectual theories and their critical rhetorics toward orthodoxy (Cohen, 2007). Furthermore the British School of IPE, "is openly normative in the tradition of pragmatism and classical moral philosophy as suggested by (Cohen, 2007 p.200). While the American School centres on the state as a central focus, the British School treats the state as only one piece of the puzzle. It, in fact, conceptualises something that is by far too complex to present itself as a more competitive form of Orthodoxy as opposed to that of the American School (Shields et al., 2011). In relation to orthodoxy on the part of the American School, the British School "or what should more appropriately be termed the British "Approach", appears to incorporate all sub-fields of IPE research. It thus opposes the positivism that is intrinsic to initial US-oriented work on governments with hegemonic stability" (Shields et al., 2011).

The British School of IPE seemed to thrive in the scholarly environment described by a free interdisciplinarity which shaped the standards of behaviour, appropriateness, outskirts, and external associations. One impression of, and centre for, this free disciplinarity and multidisciplinarity were a far-reaching recognition of, and engagement with reliable realist models with the social investigative research (Clift, 2009).   There are two concepts that Clift (2009) emphasise that separates the two school of IPE. At the point when classifying free disciplinarity, Clift maintains that British IPE "does not experience the ill effects of structures of disciplinarity that have been so evident to the American IPE (Clift, 2009). Clift likens the British School of IPE to a less intense type of order when trying to understand what is happening in the IPE which gives the impression of having a greater handle and conception.

The   British   Schools   Ontological   and Methodological investigation of IPE is not the equivalent of the American Orthodoxy approach which seems to isolate scholars in the British School. Strange and other British researchers find it challenging to publish in the United States as a result of its different methodology, which is not surprising because the British School was developed differently. The British School was established by the twentieth-century history, particular experience of that history by its defenders (Cox, 2009).

These revolutionary indicators make it feasible to, consider the possibilities of a shift in world government systems rather than being solely preoccupied with fighting for the status quo (Cox, 2009). As the Critical Theory is extremely negative of the way, American IPE academics carry out research. To the British coming up with a conclusion or making deductions in social science research is a function of, facts and data (Cox, 2009). While this might be the case, the field of the IPE continues to nourish and has now emerged into open discourses similar in scope to those of IR.

Conclusion

The field of the IPE is an individual and distinct academic area whereby scholars and students tend to focus on the often ignored bigger picture of the international political economy. Strange's great insight and ability viewed the world as one interconnected global organism.   She wrote in 1991 that the International Political Economy ought to be "an open range, like the old Wild West, accessible . . . to literate people of all walks of life, from all professions, and all political proclivities".   Throughout her professional career, she advocated against the dangers of what she saw as control of power by a limited few. Some of her notable books on this subject include *Casino Capitalism, The Retreat of the State and Mad Money.*

Strange's ideas and books led to controversies that inspired robust debates. What would become known as the first debate was between academics of the two fields of IR and the IR These scholarly debates and articles emerged in the 1970's and carried through to the 1990's. This was the catapult in getting recognition of an emerging and distinct academic discipline that is now widely taught on a global level. In the field of the International Political Economy, three separate debates have been mentioned in this paper.

The first debate is to ascertain whether the IPE is or is not a subfield of IR. This debate will probably continue to be a central issue in IPE as it progresses and finds it space as an independent discipline within the Social Science studies. Some intellectuals see IPE as nothing but a subfield of IR whereas others view IPE as a discrete school of thought. This argument of trying to determine whether the IPE is or is not a sub-field has been a continuous centrepiece of IPE.

The second debate between the Old International Political Economy (OIPE) and the New International Political Economy (NIPE). OIPE was formed in the 1970's at the height of the Cold War with the culmination of Globalisation and new international entities that were springing up around the globe. NIPE was formed towards the end of the Cold War with the collapse of the USSR in 1991 and the era of new and emerging technology and the information age. NIPE is also known as the Open Economic Politics of the 1990's. Henceforth, it should be referred to as the second great debate of IPE. It was pointed out that Open Economic Politics or New IPE is a continuation of the American vs. British School of IPE school of thought. Open Economic Politics is primarily used in American Universities and while a part of the International Political Economy delves further into areas that IPE itself seems to neglect i.e. many domestic actors, interest groups and other actors.

The third debated was initiated by the works of Benjamin Cohen who depicted the field of the International Political Economy as one that is is not unified being of two polar opposites; The American school on the western side of the Atlantic and the British school on the eastern side. Although others are denouncing and disagree with this position, one cannot deny that the two camps are uniquely different from one another.

The American School of thought has failed to progress beyond the "soothing" ideology of "complex interdependence" and has not shifted its global view from the perspective of the 70's to the "poles apart" perspective of today. A situation regretfully pointed out by Keohane (a pioneer of American IPE) is now a deserter of IPE (Shields et al., 2011). The American

School was conceived in the US as a tool for answering a set of questions of particular relevance to the US itself, specifically the problem of Hegemony and the stand of the country as the global hegemonic power (Cohen, 2008b). Thus the selfish attitude of the American approach is looked down upon by those in the British School.

The British School of IPE is different from the American School which appears to isolate scholars in the British School. The difference does not come as a shock in how the British School developed over time, but it seems to bring division among British social scientist who would like to publish their articles in the US. The British School has influenced the twentieth-century history and the personal experience of that history by its supporters (Cox, 2009) largely.

While the field of the IPE is new and some areas need more clarity regarding abbreviations and its investigation, IPE will continue to evolve into a remarkable field of research and investigation into the world economy. It will be interesting to see how these debates are perceived in IPE literature in the foreseeable future. Like its sister field, International Relations; the

International Political Economy must be regarded as a series of Great Debates that began in the 1970's.

One final thought, could there be a possible fourth debate against the Global Political Economy? Is globalisation being seen as the current downfall of nation-states i.e. mass immigration, open borders, and global terrorism? Only time will tell.

Bibliography

Amoore, L., Dodgson, R., Germain, R., Gills, B., Langley, P., & Watson., I. 2000. *Paths to a Historicized International Political Economy. Review of International Political Economy,* 7(1), 53-71. Retrieved from http://www.jstor.org/stable/4177331.

Baker A, Hudson D, & Woodward R., 2005. *Governing Financial Globalization: International Political Economy and Multi-Level Governance* (Routledge, London).

Balaam., D.N., & Dillman., B., 2016. *Introduction to International Political Economy.* Edition No 6. Published by Routledge an imprint of Taylor Francis and Group. p.1-511.

Bergsten, F.C., Keohane. R.O., & Nye, J.S., 1975. *International Economics and International Politics*: A Framework for analysis, in: F.C. Bergsten and L.B. Krause, Eds, World Politics and International Economics (Brookings, Washington).

Bernauer, T., & Achini, C., 2000. *From 'real' to 'virtual' states? Integration of the world economy and its effects on government activity.* European Journal of International Relations 6(2): 223-7.

Blyth, M. 2009. '*Torn between Two Lovers? Caught in the Middle of British and American IPE',* New Political Economy, 14(3): 329–36.

Broome, A, 2014. *Issues and Actors in the Global Political Economy.* Palgrave Macmillan. pp. 1-313.

Cameron., A., & Palan., R., 2009. *Empiricism and objectivity. Reflexive theory construction in a complex world.* In: Blyth, Mark, (ed.) *Routledge handbook of International Political Economy (IPE) IPE as a global conversation.* London; New York: Routledge, pp. 95-111. ISBN 9780415771269.

Christopher., B., 1973. *International Political Economy: Some Problems of an Inter-Disciplinary Enterprise.* International *Affairs (Royal Institute of International Affairs 1944), 49*(1), 51-60. doi:1. Retrieved from http://www.jstor.org/stable/2612905 doi:1.

Clift., B & Rosamond., B., 2009. *Lineages of a British international political economy.* In: Blyth, Mark, (ed.) *Routledge handbook of International Political Economy*

(IPE) IPE as a global conversation. London; New York: Routledge, pp. 95-111. ISBN 9780415771269.

Cohen., B. J., 2007. *The transatlantic divide: Why are American and British IPE so different? Review of International Political Economy, 14*(2), 197-219.

Cohen., B. J., 2007. *The multiple traditions of American IPE.*

Cohen., B. J, 2008a. *International Political Economy: An Intellectual History*, Princeton, NJ: Princeton University Press.

Cohen., B.J., 2008b. '*The Transatlantic Divide: A Rejoinder*', Review of International Political Economy, 15(1): 30-4.

Cohen., B.J., 2010. *Are IPE Journals Becoming Boring?* International Studies Quarterly, 54, 887-891.

Cox., R., 1981. *In search of international political economy a review essay,* New Political Science, 2:1-2, 59-78, DOI: 10.1080/07393148108429521.

Cox., R. 1986. *'Social forces, states, and world orders: beyond international relations theory'.* In Robert O

Keohane (ed), Neorealism and its critics New York: Columbia University, pp. 204-54.

Cox., R.W., 1996. *Social Forces, States and World Order: Beyond International Relations Theory* (1981) in R.W. Cox and T.J. Sinclair (eds.), Approaches to World Order, Cambridge: Cambridge University Press, pp. 85-123.

Cox., R.W., 2009. Special Symposium. *The British School in The Global Context.* New Political Economy. Vol.14. No. 3, September 2009.

Denemark, R., & O'Brien, R., 1997. *Contesting the Canon: International Political Economy at UK and US Universities. Review of International Political Economy,* 4(1), 214-238. Retrieved from http://www.jstor.org/stable/4177220.

Dickins, A., 2006. *The evolution of the international political economy.* International Affairs, 82(3), 479-492.

Eichengreen, B., 1998. '*Dental hygiene and nuclear war: How international relations looks at economics',* International Organization, 52 (4): 993-1012.

Farrell, H., & Finnemore, M. 2009. *Ontology, methodology, and causation in the American school of international political economy. Review of International Political Economy, 16,* 58–71.

Farrell H and Newman A. 2014. *Domestic institutions beyond the nation state: Charting the new interdependence approach.* World Politics 65(2): forthcoming.

Frieden, J.A., & Martin, L, L., 2001. *International Political Economy: The state of the sub-discipline.* p. 1-53.

Frieden, J. A., & Martin, L, L., 2002. *"International Political Economy: Global and Domestic Interactions."* In Political Science: The State of the Discipline, Ed. Ira Katznelson and Helen V. Milner. New York: W. W. Norton for the American Political Science Association, 118–46.

Frieden, Jeffry A., & Lake David A., 2003. *International Political Economy. Perspectives on Global Power and Wealth.* Routledge, fourth edition. p.1-496.

Frieden, Jeffry A., & Martin L. L., 2001. *"International Political Economy: The state of the sub-discipline." Manuscript, Harvard University, Cambridge, MA, Department of Government* (2001). p.1-53

Frieden, J.A. & Martin, L. L. (2003). *International political economy: global and domestic interactions.* Pp. 118–46 in *Political Science: The State of the Discipline,* ed. I. Katznelson and H. V. Milner. New York: W. W. Norton for the American Political Science Association.

Garrett, G., 1998a. Partisan Politics in the Global Economy. Cambridge: Cambridge University Press.

Germain, R., D., 2009. *The American School of IP? A dissenting view.* Review of International Political Economy. Volume 16, Issue 1. p. 95-105.

Germann, J. 2011. *International Political Economy and the Crises of the 1970s: The Real 'Transatlantic Divide'.* Journal: Journal of Critical Globalization Studies (JCGS) ISSN 2040-8498 Volume: 1; Issue: 4.

Gill, B., 2001. *Re-orienting the New (International) Political Economy.* New Political Economy, Vol 6, No. 2

Gill, S. R., & Law D., 1989. *Global Hegemony and the Structural Power of Capital.* International Studies Quarterly 33:475–99.

Gill, S. R., & Law D., 1989. *The Global Political Economy – Perspectives, Problems, and Policies.* Harvester Wheatsheaf, 1998, p.7.

Gilpin, R. (1975b) U.S. Power and the Multinational Corporation, New York: Basic Books.

Gilpin, R., 1987. *The Political Economy of International Relations.* Princeton University Press. p. xvi, 449.

Gilpin, R., 2001. *Global Political Economy: Understanding the International Economic Order,* Princeton University Press, Princeton.

Hay, C., & Marsh., D. 1999. *Introduction: Towards a new (international) political economy?* New Political Economy, 4:1, 5-22, DOI: 10.1080/13563469908406382

Higgott, R., & Watson, M., 2008. *All at Sea in a Barbed-Wire Canoe: Professor Cohen's Transatlantic Voyage in IPE. Review of International Political Economy, 15*(1), 1-17. Retrieved from http://www.jstor.org/stable/25261951

Hirst., P., & Thompson, G., 1996. *GLOBALIZATION IN QUESTION: THE INTERNATIONAL ECONOMY AND THE POSSIBILITIES OF GOVERNANCE.* Polity Press, Cambridge.

Hobson., J.M. 2013. *Part 2 – Reconstructing the non-Eurocentric foundations of IPE*: From Eurocentric 'open economy politics' to inter-civilizational political economy, Review of International Political Economy, 20:5, 1055-1081, DOI: 10.1080/09692290.2012.733498

Hveem., H, 2009. *Pluralist IPE: A View from Outside the 'Schools'*, New Political Economy, 14:3, 367-376, DOI: 10.1080/13563460903087516

Jackson R., & Sorenson, G., 2002. *Introduction to International Relations Theories and Approaches.* Oxford University Press, p. 178.

Jones, R. 1982. *International Political Economy: Perspectives and Prospects: Part II. Review of International Studies, 8*(1), 39-52. Retrieved from http://www.jstor.org/stable/20096936.

Keating, M.F., Kuzemko, C., Belyi, A.V. and Goldthau, A., 2012. *Introduction: Bringing energy into the international political economy.* In *Dynamics of Energy Governance in Europe and Russia* (pp. 1-19). Palgrave Macmillan UK.

Keohane, R.O., 2009. '*The old IPE and the new*', *Review of International Political Economy,* Vol. 16, No. 1, pp.34–46.

Lake, D.A., 2008. *International Political Economy: A North American Perspective on an Emerging Interdiscipline. world.*

Lake, D.A., 2009. *TRIPs across the Atlantic: Theory and epistemology in IPE. Review of International Political Economy, 16*(1), pp.47-57.

Lake, D.A., 2009b. '*Open Economy Politics: A Critical Review*', *Review of International Organizations,* 4(3): 219-44.

Langley, P., 2003. *World financial orders: an historical international political economy*. Routledge.

Leiteritz, Ralf J. (2005*). INTERNATIONAL POLITICAL ECONOMY: The state of the art*. Colombia Internacional, (62), 50-63. Retrieved December 03, 2015, from http://www.scielo.org.co/scielo.php?script=sci_arttext&p id=S0121-56122005000200004&lng=en&tlng=en

Lim, Timothy., C. 2014. *International Political Economy – An Introduction to Approaches, Regimes, and Issues.*

The Open Text Book Challenge. The Saylor Foundation. p.1-448.

Maliniak, D., & Tierney, M. J. 2009. *The American school of IPE. Review of International Political Economy, 16*(1), 6-33.

Morrison, K. M. 2011. *"Nontax Revenue, Social Cleavages, and Authoritarian Stability in Mexico and Kenya: 'Internationalization, Institutions, and Political Change' Revisited."* Comparative Political Studies 44, no. 6: 719 –46.

Mosley, L., 2005. *Globalization and the state: still room to move?* New Political Economy 10(3): 355-62.

Mosley, L. & Singer, D. 2009. *The global financial crisis.* Int. Interact. 35(4):420–29

Mosley, L. & Singer, D., 2010. *The Global Financial Crisis: Lessons and Opportunities for International Political Economy.* In N. Phillips & C. Weaver (Eds.), International Political Economy: Debating the Past, Present and Future. London: Routledge.

Milner, H. V. 1998. *International political economy: Beyond hegemonic stability. Foreign Policy,* (110), 112-123. Retrieved from:

http://search.proquest.com/docview/224055285?accounti
d=12253

Miller, R. C. 2008. *International Political Economy: Contrasting World Views.* London: Routledge.

Murphy, C.N. And Nelson, D.R., 2001. *International political economy: a tale of two heterodoxies.* The British Journal of Politics and International Relations, *3* (3), pp. 393-412.

Oatley, T., 2011. *The reductionist gamble: Open economy politics in the global economy. International Organization,* 65(02), pp.311-341.

O'Brien, R. & Williams, M. 2013. *GLOBAL POLITICAL ECONOMY: EVOLUTION AND DYNAMICS.* Published by PALGRAVE MACMILLAN. 4th ed.

Pevehouse, J., & Jason B., 2008. 'Time-series analysis', in Janet BoxSteffensmeier, Henry Brady, and David Collier (eds) The Oxford Handbook of Political Methodology, Oxford: Oxford University Press, pp. 456–474.

Paul, D. & Amawi, A. 2013. *The Theoretical Evolution of International Political Economy,* Third Edition: A Reader. New York: Oxford University Press.

Rho, S., & Tomz, M. 2016. *"Why Don't Trade Preferences Reflect Economic Self-Interest?"* Manuscript At   http://web.stanford.edu/~tomz/work   ing/RhoTomz-2016-06-01.pdf, Accessed on 19 January 2017.

Owen., E., & Walter., S., 2016. *OPEN ECONOMY POLITICS AND BREXIT: INSIGHTS, PUZZLES AND WAYS FORWARD*. Working paper. 2016. Pp. 1-22.

Pepinsky, T. B. 2013. *"Surveys, Experiments, and the Landscape of International Political Economy."* Working paper, Department of Government, Cornell University. Pp. 1-13.

Ravenhill, J., 2009. International Political Economy. *Oxford Handbooks Online.* Retrieved 7 Dec. 2015, from, http://www.oxfordhandbooks.com/view/10.1093/oxfordh b/9780199219322.001.0001/oxfordhb-9780199219322-e-31

RIPE Editors., 1994. '*Editorial: Forum for Heterodox International Political Economy*', Review of International Political Economy, 1 (1): 1–12.

Samman, A. and Seabrooke, L. (2016) International Political Economy, in X.Guillaume, P. Bilgin and M.B.

Salter   (eds.)
Routledge Handbook of InternationalPolitical Sociology, London: Routledge, in press.

Sharmen, J.C. & Weaver, C. 2013. Ripe, The American School, and diversity in Global IPE. Review of International Political Economy. Vol. 20, Iss. 5.

Shields, S., Bruff, I. & Macartney, H. (Eds.). 2011. *Critical International Political Economy*. Basingstoke, UK: Palgrave.

Smith, S. 1995. *'The Self-Image of a Discipline: A Genealogy of International Relations Theory'*, in K. Booth and S. Smith (Eds), International Relations Theory Today (Cambridge).

Spero, J.E., 1977. The Politics of International Economic Relations. London. Allen & Unwin.

Stephens, JD., Huber, E., & Ray L. 1999. The welfare state in hard times. In: Kitschelt H, Lange P, Marks G and Stephens JD (eds) Continuity and Change in Contemporary Capitalism. Cambridge: Cambridge University Press.

Strange, S., 1970. *International Economics and International Relations: A Case of Mutual Neglect.* International Affairs, 46, 304-315.

Strange, S. 1991. *An Eclectic Approach*, in C. N. Murphy and R. Tooze, eds The New International Political Economy (Basingstoke: Macmillan)

Strange, S. 1994. States and markets. Reprint of 2nd ed. pub. by Pinter, 1994; previous ed. 1988. 266p : ill. ; 23 cm. London : Continuum,

Strange, S., 1996. *'A Reply to Chris May, Global Society,* Vo. .10, No.3, (1996) p. .303-5. In reply to Chris May, 'Strange Fruit: Susan Strange's theory of Structural Power in the International Political Economy, Global Society, Vol.10, No.2 pp. 167-189.

Strange, S. ed., 2010. *Paths to International Political Economy (Routledge Revivals).* Routledge.

Telo, M., 2009. *International Relations: A European Perspective.* Routledge Taylor and Francis Group. New York, NY. p. 1-223.

Tooze, R., 1984. *'In search of "international political economy"'.* Political Studies XXXII: 637 46.

Tooze, R., 1996. *The After-Shock of the 'Neo': Agendas of IPE and IR. Review of International Political Economy, 3*(1), 194-204. Retrieved from http://www.jstor.org/stable/4177181.

Tooze, R., 2000. *Susan Strange, Academic International Relations and the Study of International Political Economy*, New Political Economy, 5:2, 280-289, DOI: 10.1080/713687770.

Underhill, Gooffrey R.D. 2000. State, Market and Global Politcal Economy. Genealogy of an (Inter?) Discipline," International Affairs, 76:4 (October) 805-824.

Verdun, A., 2003. *An American/European divide in European integration studies: bridging the gap with international political economy.* Journal of European Public Policy, 10:1, 84- Walter, A., Sen, G., & Cohen, B., 2009. *International Political Economy. In Analyzing the Global Political Economy* (pp. 1-26). Princeton University Press. Retrieved from http://www.jstor.org/stable/j.ctt7swg3.7101, DOI: 10.1080/1350176032000046958.

Weaver, C., 2008. *Reflections on the American School: An IPE of our making.* Review of International Political Economy. 16:1. p.1-5.

Weaver, C., 2009. *IPE's Split Brain.* New Political Economy. Vol. 14, Issue 3. p.337-346.

Woods, N., 2008. *The Globalization of World Politics: an Introduction to International.* Oxford University Press.